Jorge Gómez
Velssy Hernández

TEACHING NEURAL NETWORK PROGRAMMING

Jorge Gómez
Velssy Hernández

TEACHING NEURAL NETWORK PROGRAMMING

Designing and implementing neural networks from scratch

ScienciaScripts

Imprint
Any brand names and product names mentioned in this book are subject to trademark, brand or patent protection and are trademarks or registered trademarks of their respective holders. The use of brand names, product names, common names, trade names, product descriptions etc. even without a particular marking in this work is in no way to be construed to mean that such names may be regarded as unrestricted in respect of trademark and brand protection legislation and could thus be used by anyone.

Cover image: www.ingimage.com

This book is a translation from the original published under ISBN 978-3-639-64602-3.

Publisher:
Sciencia Scripts
is a trademark of
Dodo Books Indian Ocean Ltd. and OmniScriptum S.R.L publishing group

120 High Road, East Finchley, London, N2 9ED, United Kingdom
Str. Armeneasca 28/1, office 1, Chisinau MD-2012, Republic of Moldova, Europe
Printed at: see last page
ISBN: 978-620-7-74506-7

TEACHING NEURAL NETWORK PROGRAMMING

JORGE GOMEZ GOMEZ
VELSSY HERNÁNDEZ RIAÑO

TEACHING NEURAL NETWORK PROGRAMMING

Designing and implementing neural networks from scratch

JORGE GOMEZ GOMEZ
VELSSY HERNÁNDEZ RIAÑO

ABOUT THE AUTHORS:

Jorge Gómez Gómez
Systems Engineer by profession graduated from Fundación Universitaria San Martín, Master in Telematics Engineering from Universidad del Cauca, PhD in Information Technology and Communications from the University of Granada Spain, full time professor of Systems Engineering at the University of Cordoba. Director of the SOCRATES research group of the Systems Engineering program at the University of Cordoba, Editor-in-Chief of the Engineering and Innovation magazine of the University of Cordoba. Member and founder of the IEEE student branch of the University of Cordoba. I have published numerous articles in the area of Internet of Things, Context Awareness, e-learning, telecommunications networks, in different journals indexed in JCR and SCOPUS indexes. I have developed research projects related to citizen security, smart cities, Internet of Things for health issues, among others. I am the coordinator of the Pervasive Computing research group of the Systems Engineering program at the University of Córdoba. In this research group we develop research activities oriented to intelligent systems based on technologies such as RFID, NFC, QRCODE, geolocation systems, ubiquitous and pervasive systems. Also in this seedbed students propose solutions in the above mentioned topics; members actively participate inside and outside the university in research activities. As a result, many members have won regional and national awards. In addition, I have participated as a jury evaluator of indexed journals, master's and doctoral theses. I am also guest editor of the journal Computational and Mathematical Methods in Medicine-Hindawi. I have been a guest professor at the Corporación Universitaria de la Costa, in the PhD program in Information and Communication Technologies, in the subject Semantic Representation of Information in Ubiquitous Environments. I have been a professor at the Universidad Cooperativa de Colombia in Monteria from 2008 to 2015, where I taught courses in artificial intelligence, databases and telecommunications networks. Similarly, I was a professor at the Universidad del Sinú from 2008 to 2015, where I was also director of the GNOCIX research group of the Systems Engineering career. I have been a speaker at national and international events. At the international level I was invited by the State Technical University of Quevedo Ecuador to give a seminar on Internet of Things in 2014. In 2016 I was invited by the University of Babahoyo Ecuador to give a workshop seminar on Ubiquitous Systems. I have participated in internal calls for research at the University of Cordoba, as well as in external calls such as Minciencias.

Finally I can say that with the experience I have had over the years as a professional, I have contributed to generate new knowledge, this has been reflected in the articles I have published, the graduate work I have directed, the courses I have taught and the appropriation of knowledge to the educational community. Within the IEEE Branch of the University of Cordoba, I have promoted research and social projection of knowledge to social environments that have required it.

Velssy Hernández Riaño:
She is a Systems Engineer and holds a Master's degree in Telematics Engineering from Universidad Francisco José de Caldas, Colombia. She is a Professor and Researcher of the SOCRATES research group of the Systems Engineering Department of the University of Córdoba.

CONTENTS

INTRODUCTION

Deep learning is an area of artificial intelligence that deals with the use of computational models to solve highly complex problems that require precision in their results. Within this line of deep learning, we find deep belief networks, Autoencoders, RBM systems or Boltzmann Constraint Machines, Recurrent Neural Networks RNN, and Convolutional Neural Networks CNN.

Within the uses of Deep Learning, we find countless applications, ranging from recommendation systems used by platforms such as Netflix, Youtube, Facebook and others. We also find applications for autonomous driving systems for object and pedestrian detection, health care (cancer detection from images), DNA decoding, facial recognition, security and surveillance, etc.

Neural networks are part of this family of deep learning, which are applied to the solution of various problems that require a high degree of complexity and precision in the outputs. In this book we briefly address the theoretical foundation of neural networks, from the basic principles of how a neuron works and its similarity with the biological part, which explains its axons (inputs), the weights of the inputs, the bias, the body of the neuron, the activation function and the output function of the axon. Subsequently, the architecture of a multilayer neural network, the learning process of the neural network through the functions of backpropagation and feedforward propagation are described.

Finally, the book proceeds to train a neural network from scratch, with the objective of teaching the reader in a simple way how to design a neural network and the processes involved in learning it. Subsequently, a problem is defined for the detection of the late blight pest in potato crops. The theoretical foundation of a convolutional network and definitions related to potato blight are presented. The reader is then presented with a step-by-step guide on how to create a project in Jupyter-lab for the detection of potato leaf blight. Initially it is explained how to train and save the model and then the reader is shown how to use the model by developing a web application that consumes the pre-trained model. At the end the reader can program all the routines step by step and verify through the final application, the usefulness of the model. The reader is left with an exercise to use the template to train the model and do the same for the detection of the same pest in pepper leaves.

In general terms, this book is very succinct in nature, but it teaches the basics so that a person with a background in mathematics, statistics and programming can enter the world of deep learning without any difficulty. It is important to give credit to the developers of working environments such as Jupyter-lab, Notebook, Pandas, Anaconda and the Sklearn libraries, because thanks to these contributions, artificial intelligence research projects can be done much more easily and quickly. Contrary to previous decades, where the learning curve of these models and tools were too complex and difficult to implement.

Theoretical basis
What is a neural network?

Artificial neural networks are popular machine learning techniques that mimic the learning process of living beings. In the human nervous system, cells called neurons are interconnected through axons and dendrites, and the areas of connection are known as synapses. These synapses are essential, as they represent the neural connections, whose strength can change in response to external stimuli, which facilitates learning in living beings. This biological process is replicated in artificial neural networks, where processing units, called neurons, are linked by weights that play a role similar to that of synaptic connections in living organisms (Goldberg,2016; Acharya et al.,2017).

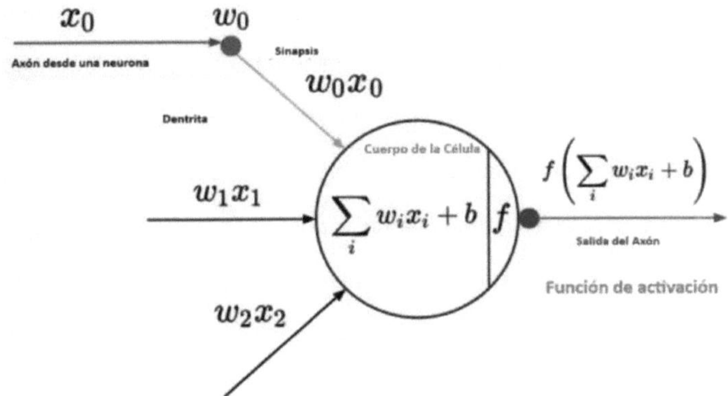

Figure 1. Architecture of a neuron - adapted from https://pub.towardsai.net/neural-network-from-scratch-6fa1e78a3515 .

Each input signal arriving at a neuron is modified by a value called a weight, which influences the function that computes that neuron. This arrangement is shown in Figure 1. An artificial neural network performs computations from the inputs, propagating the results from the input neurons to the output neurons, and using the weights as intermediate variables (Grossberg and Merrill, 1992).

The learning process involves adjusting these weights that connect neurons, similar to how biological organisms need external stimuli to learn. In the case of artificial neural networks, these external stimuli are provided by training data, which consist of examples of input-output pairs of the function to be learned. For example, the training set may contain images represented in pixels (input) and corresponding labels (e.g., images of healthy and diseased tomatoes) as output.

These data pairs are used to train the neural network, which then makes predictions about the output labels from the input representations. During training, the data provide feedback on the accuracy of the weights in the neural network, based on how well the predictions match the output labels annotated in the training data. The neurons adjust their weights in response to prediction errors, with the goal of modifying the computed function to improve accuracy in future iterations. This adjustment of the weights is performed in a careful and mathematically justified manner, with the purpose of minimizing the error in the calculations (Nagabandi et al., 2018).

As the weights between neurons are successively adjusted using multiple input-output pairs, the function computed by the neural network is refined over time, resulting in more accurate predictions. This process allows the neural network to generalize its ability to make accurate predictions on new inputs that it has not seen before, such as correctly identifying a tomato in an image that was not part of the original training set. This ability of the neural network to make accurate predictions about inputs not seen during training is known as model generalization (Schmidhuber, 2015).

Basic architecture of a neural network

In the single-layer network, a set of inputs is mapped directly to an output through the use of a variation. The minimal expression of a neural network is known as a perceptron, as shown in Figure 2.

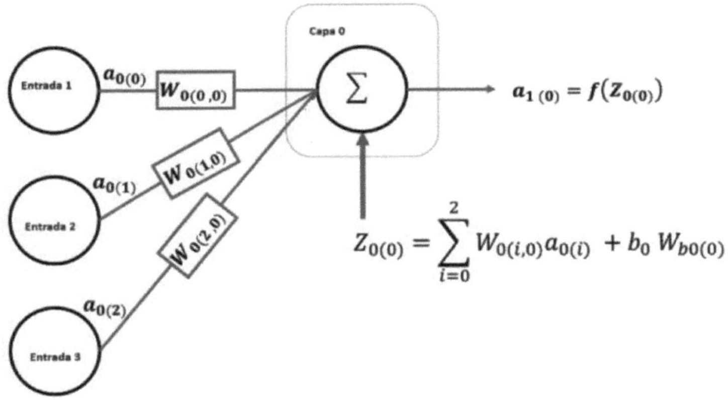

Figure 2. Perceptron without bias.

The structure of the perceptron, depicted in Figure 2, consists of a single input layer that transmits the features to the output node. On the links from the input to the output are the weights w0...wn, which multiply the features and are summed at the output node (Schmidhuber, 2015).

Then, an activation function, such as the sign function, is used to convert the resulting value into a class label. This activation function is crucial in the process

11

and may vary according to the type of machine learning model to be simulated, such as least squares or softmax regression, among others. One of the most common activation functions in neural networks is the sigmoid function, illustrated in Figure 3.

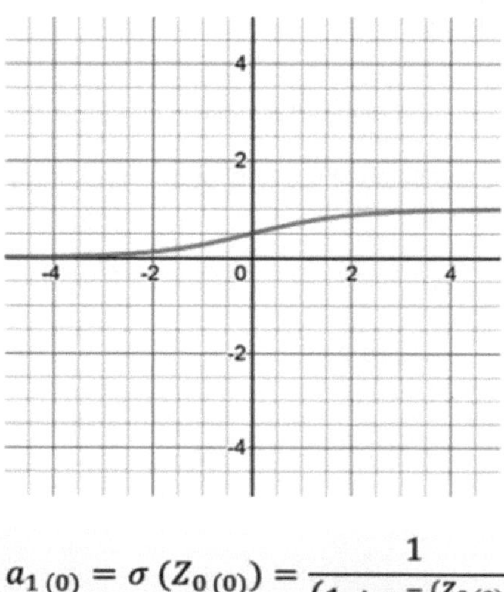

$$a_{1\,(0)} = \sigma\left(Z_{0\,(0)}\right) = \frac{1}{\left(1 + e^{-\left(Z_{0\,(0)}\right)}\right)}$$

Figure 3. Bias with sigmoid function.

Most elementary machine learning models can be easily visualized as simple neural network configurations. This practice is useful for representing traditional machine learning methods in terms of neural architectures, as it provides a clearer understanding of how deep learning extends the scope of conventional machine learning. The input layer is not counted within the total number of layers in a neural network. Since the perceptron consists of only one processing layer, it is classified as a single-layer network (Nielsen, 2015).

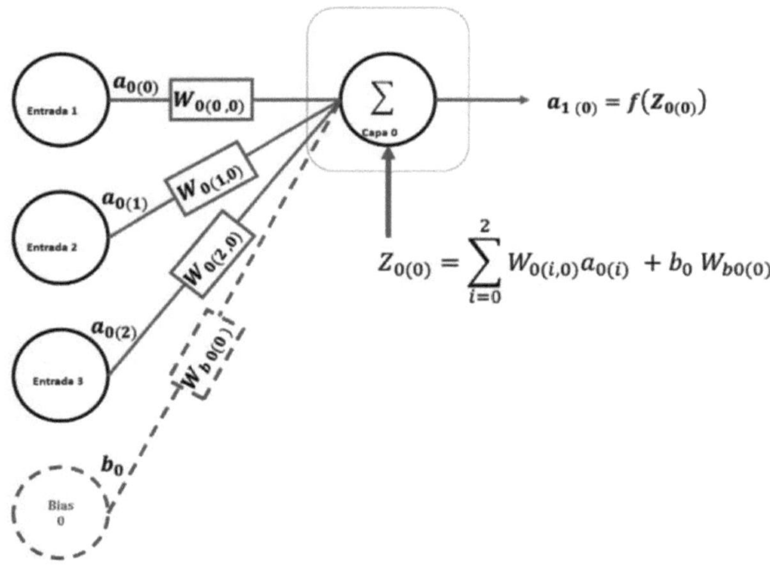

Figure 4. Biased Perceptron

In several models, there is a constant part of the prediction known as bias. To capture this invariant part of the prediction, it is required to include an additional bias variable, represented by "b". This bias can be incorporated as an additional weight on the edge by using a bias neuron. This is achieved by adding a neuron that always outputs a value of 1 towards the output node (Schmidhuber, 2015). The edge weight connecting the bias neuron to the output node provides the bias variable, as illustrated in Figure 4.

Next, a neural network problem will be presented graphically based on the need of a person to travel to a specific destination, for this purpose some conditions must be met, such as:

X1: Do you have enough money? 1/0

X2: Does your family want to go on a trip? 1/0

X3: Is the place nice? 1/0

Figure 5 shows the initial conditions.

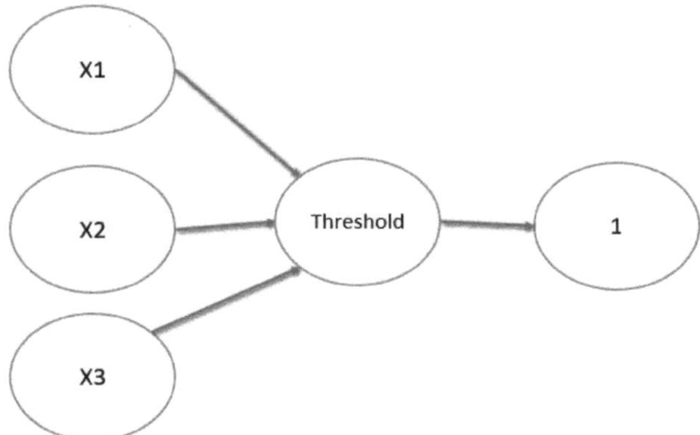

Figure 5. Initial conditions

Now, in order to make the decision to go on a trip, the input parameters must be above the threshold, so that the input data must be greater than the threshold, as shown in Figure 6.

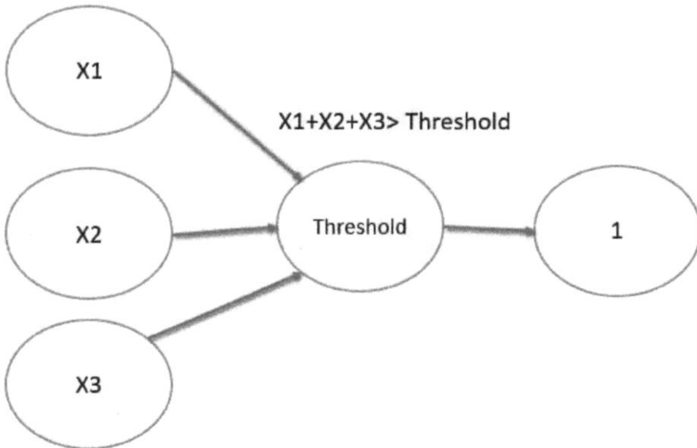

Figure 6. Definition of the threshold in the neural network.

Next, in Figures 7 and 8, we will play with the condition factors, such as that condition one is met, i.e., he has enough money to travel, and condition three, that the place is nice, regardless of the family not wanting to travel, which would

be condition two.

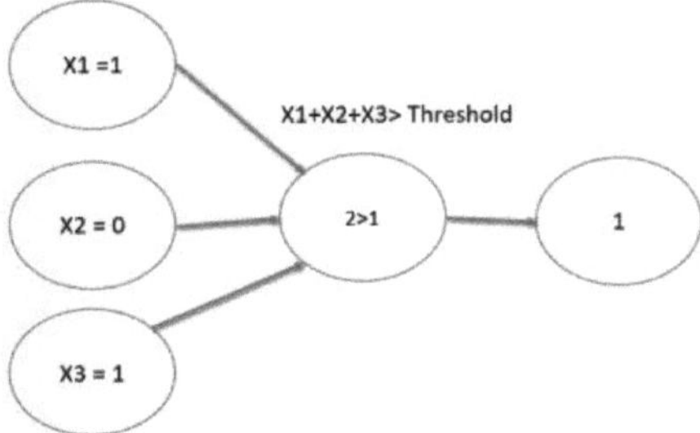

Figure 7. You have enough money and the place is nice.

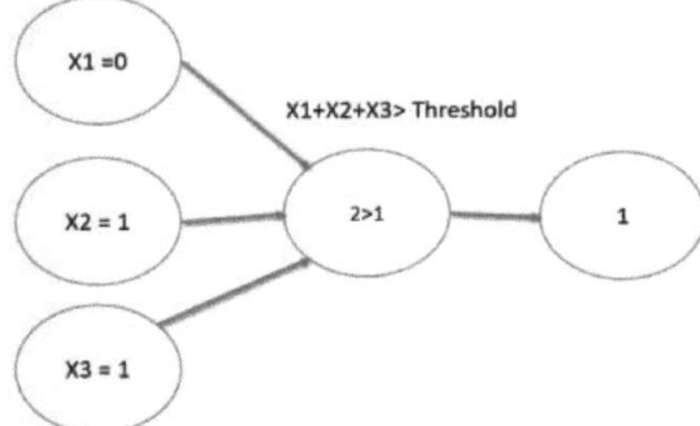

Figure 8. The family wants to go on a trip and the place is nice.

Note that in Figure 8, the person does not have enough money, so a question

arises, how is he going to travel if he has no money? This is a very good question.

One way to solve it, is to define some weights for each input, so that, based on

these weights, the activation function can be executed. Following the example,

as seen in Figure 9, for this problem, a higher weight is given to money enough

to travel. It makes sense, if you have money, you could travel, either without your

family or if the place is not nice.

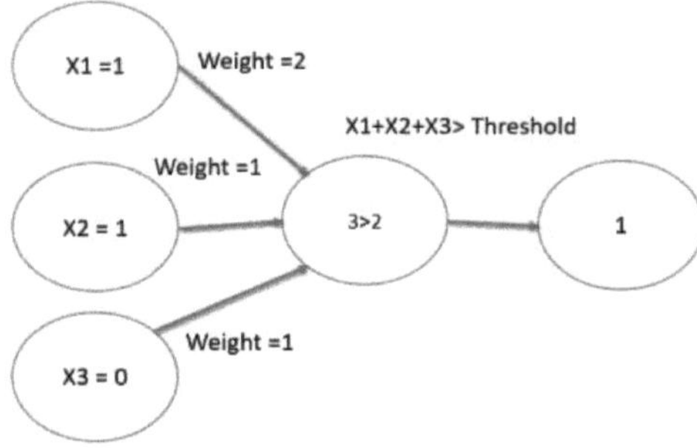

Figure 9. A greater weight is given to variable X1.

Next, continuing with the input combinations and weights, we can observe the behaviors of the activation function in Figures 10, 11 and 12.

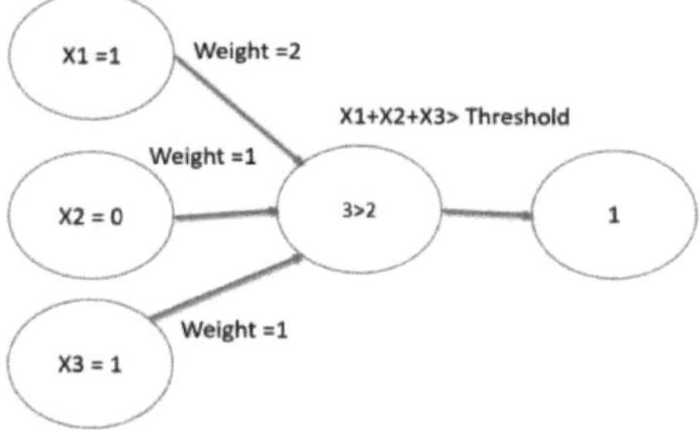

Figure 10. You have enough money and the place is nice.

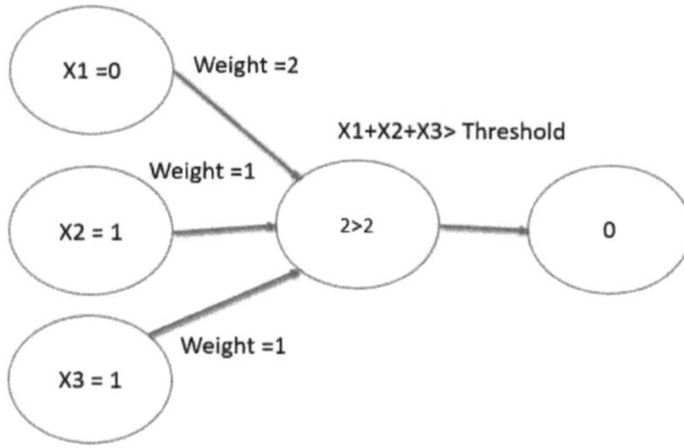

Figure 11. The place is nice and the family wants to travel

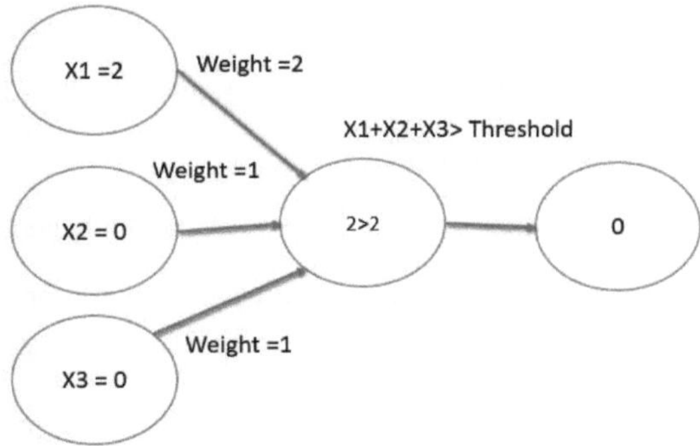

Figure 12. You have money to travel, but the family does not want to travel and the place is unpleasant.

As can be seen in Figure 11, even though the family wants to travel and the place is pleasant, the weight of the input variable availability of sufficient money is not met, obviously it is not possible to travel. And in Figure 12, there is enough money, but the family does not want to travel and the place is unpleasant, therefore, it is a sufficient reason for not going on a trip.

In summary:

- Output: This is the final value or activation of the neuron.
- Activation_function: this is a mathematical function that determines whether the neuron should be activated or not depending on its input.
- Weighted_sum: This is the sum of the products of the input values and their corresponding weights.
- Bias: a bias term is added to the weighted sum to provide the neuron with some flexibility in its activation.

The weighted sum is calculated as follows: weighted_sum = (w1 * x1) + (w2 * x2) + ... + (wn * xn) Where: w1, w2, ..., wn: these are the weights associated with each input.x1, x2, ..., xn: these are the input values.

The activation function can be any nonlinear function, such as sigmoid function, ReLU (Rectified Linear Unit) or softmax, depending on the type of neuron and the task at hand.

Multilayer neural networks

Multilayer neural networks consist of more than one processing layer. In the case of the perceptron, it consists of an input layer and an output layer, the latter being in charge of performing the computations. The input layer transmits the data to the output layer, where all calculations are visible to the user. However, in multilayer neural networks, additional intermediate layers are added between the input and output, known as hidden layers, since the computations performed in them are not directly observable by the user, as shown in Figure 13.

The specific structure of multilayer neural networks is called feedback networks, because successive layers communicate with each other in a unidirectional direction from the input to the output. The default configuration of feedback networks assumes that all nodes in one layer are connected to those in the next layer. Therefore, once the number of layers and the number/type of nodes in each layer are defined, the architecture of the neural network is practically determined. The only remaining aspect is the loss function that is optimized in the output layer. Although the perceptron algorithm employs the perceptron criterion, there are several options (Montesinos et al., 2022). It is very common to use cross-entropy lossy softmax outputs for discrete predictions and squared-loss linear outputs for real-valued predictions.

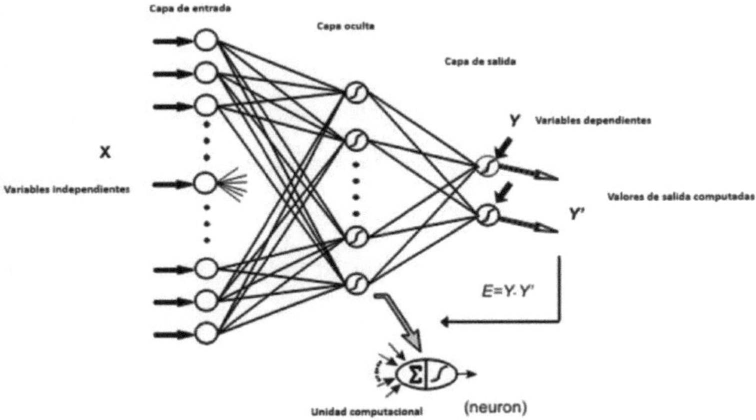

Figure 13. Multilayer neural network model taken from (Park and Lek, 2016).

Operation of a neural network

Training of a neural network with backpropagation (Backpropagation)

In a single-layer neural network, the training process is quite simple, since the error or loss function can be calculated directly from the weights, which facilitates the computation of the gradient. However, in the case of multilayer neural networks, a challenge arises because the loss is a complex function of the composition of the weights in the previous layers. To address this problem, the backpropagation algorithm, which is based on the chain rule of differential calculus, is used. This algorithm calculates error gradients in terms of sums of products of local gradients along the different paths from a node to the output (Cilimkovic, 2015; Baldi et al.,

19

2018). Although this sum involves an exponential number of components (paths), it can be efficiently computed by dynamic programming, as shown in Figure 14. The backpropagation algorithm is based on dynamic programming and consists of two main phases: the forward phase, which is responsible for calculating the output values and local derivatives at several nodes, and the reverse phase, which accumulates the products of these local values over all paths from the node to the output.

During the direct phase of the training process of a neural network, inputs corresponding to a training instance are entered. This generates a direct sequence of calculations between the layers using the current weights. The final predicted output can be compared with the actual output of the training instance, and the derivative of the loss function with respect to the output is calculated. Subsequently, in the inverse phase, it is necessary to calculate the derivative of this loss with respect to the weights in all layers. This step is usually the most challenging part of most machine learning algorithms. A significant contribution of the neural network approach is the introduction of the concept of modularity in machine learning (Liao et al., 2018).

In a single-layer neural network, the training process is relatively simple, since the error or loss function can be calculated directly from the weights, which facilitates the calculation of the gradient. However, in the case of multilayer networks, a challenge arises because the loss is a complex function of the composition of the weights in the previous layers.

To address this problem, the backpropagation algorithm, which takes advantage of the chain rule of differential calculus, is used. This algorithm computes error gradients in terms of sums of products of local gradients along the different paths from a node to the output. Although this sum involves an exponential number of components, it can be computed efficiently by dynamic programming (Hecht- et al., 1992). The backpropagation algorithm consists of two main phases:

- The forward phase, necessary to calculate the output values and local derivatives at several nodes -

- The backtracking phase, necessary to accumulate the products of these local values on all paths from the node to the output.

The backtracking phase is mainly focused on learning the gradient of the loss function in relation to the different weights using the chain rule of differential calculus. These gradients are used to adjust the weights. Since this learning process proceeds in reverse, starting from the output node, it is referred to as the backward phase (Badr, 2021).

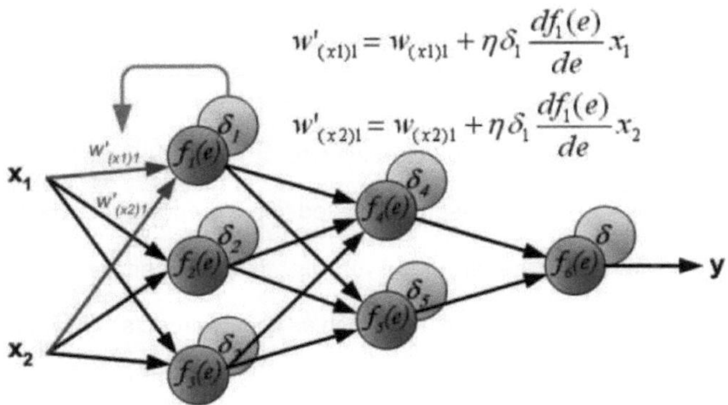

Figure 14. Backpropagation method taken from (http://galaxy.agh.edu.pl/~vlsi/AI/backp_t_en/backprop.html)

Training of a neural network with direct feedforward propagation

The training process of a neural network with direct feedforward propagation is essential in the field of deep learning. These neural networks are composed of an input layer, at least one hidden layer and an output layer (Ozanich et al., 2020; Khan et al., 2023). Each node in the network is connected to nodes in adjacent layers by corresponding weights and thresholds. Figure 15 shows how this process works.

How does direct propagation work in neural networks?

Direct propagation in a neural network is the process by which input data traverse the different layers of the network to generate an output. This process involves the following steps:

1. Input layer: The input data is fed into the initial layer of the neural network.
2. Hidden layers: Input data are processed through one or more hidden layers. Each neuron in a hidden layer receives inputs from the previous layer, applies an activation function to the weighted sum of these inputs and transmits the result to the next layer.
3. Output layer: The processed data is fed to the output layer, where the final network output is generated. Typically, this layer applies an activation function appropriate for the task, such as softmax for classification or linear activation for regression.

4. Prediction: The final output of the neural network represents the prediction or classification of the input data. Forward propagation is crucial for making these predictions in neural networks. It calculates the output of the network for a specific input based on the current values of the weights and biases. This output is then compared with the actual target value to calculate the loss, which is used to update the weights and biases during the training process.

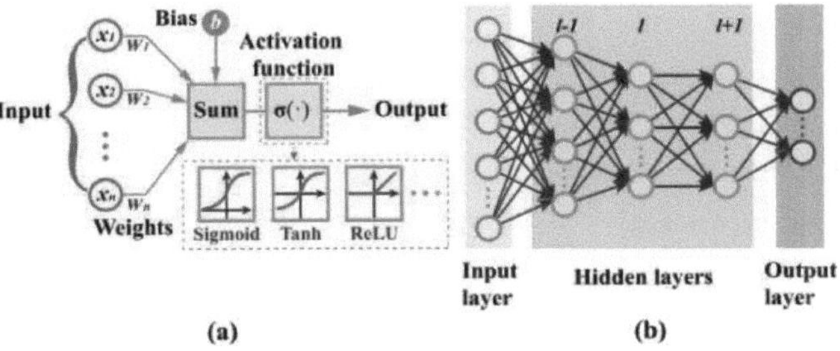

(a)   (b)

Figure 15. Direct propagation method taken from (Ma and Mei, 2021).

Training a neural network from scratch

The purpose of the neural network is to predict whether a binary number has an odd or even number with the value of one, as shown in Figure 16.

A	B	C	Y
0	0	0	0
0	0	1	1
0	1	0	1
0	1	1	0
1	0	0	1
1	0	1	0
1	1	0	0
1	1	1	1

Figure 16. X-OR operator

Next, we will open a new project in jupyter-lab

Add the following line of code

```
#Importamos la libreria numpy para la gestión de vectores
import numpy as np
```

Click on the run button

Next, we will define the independent variables in X and the dependent variable in
Y. Add the following code:

```
#Definiendo las variables dependientes
X= np.array(([0,0,0],
        [0,0,1],
        [0,1,0],
        [0,1,1],
        [1,0,0],
        [1,0,1],
        [1,1,0],
        [1,1,1]), dtype = float)
#Definiendo la variable dependiente
y= np.array((([0],
        [1],
        [1],
        [0],
        [1],
        [0],


[0],
        [1]), dtype = float)
```

Click on run

Next, we will show the values of the independent variables, stored in X, add the
following line of code:

```
print (X)
```

Click on the run button

It should look something like this:

```
[[0. 0. 0.]
 [0. 0. 1.]
 [0. 1. 0.]
 [0. 1. 1.]
 [1. 0. 0.]
 [1. 0. 1.]
 [1. 1. 0.]
 [1. 1. 1.]]
```

Which is equal to the data expressed in Figure 16.

Next, we will show the values of the dependent variable Y

Add the following line of code:

```
print (y)
```

Click on the run button, it should look something like this:

```
[[0.]
 [1.]
 [1.]
 [0.]
 [1.]
 [0.]
 [0.]
 [1.]]
```

Displays the values entered in the variable Y

Next, we will define the weights, the outputs of layer 0 and the output of the neural network.

Add the following lines of code:

```
lr = 0.5 #Tasa de aprendizaje

w0 = np.random.randn(X.shape[1],4)

w1 = np.random.randn(4,1)

output = np.zeros(y.shape)

Z0,z1,a0,a1,a2,error = [],[],[],[],[],[]
```

Click on the run button

Next, we will program the sigmoid function in Figure 17.

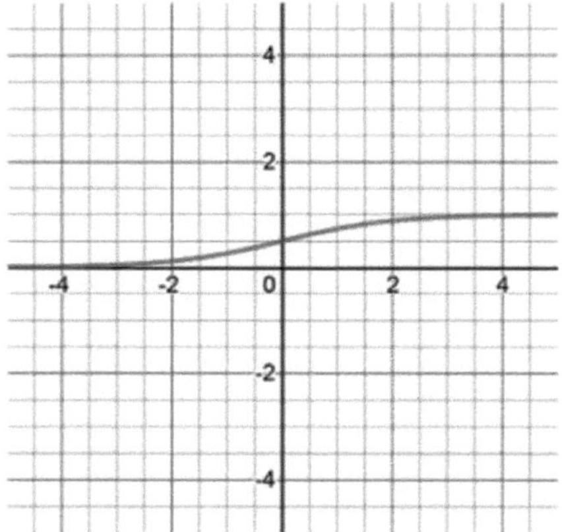

$$a_{1\,(0)} = \sigma\left(Z_{0\,(0)}\right) = \frac{1}{\left(1 + e^{-\left(Z_{0\,(0)}\right)}\right)}$$

Figure 17. Sigmoid function.

Then add the following line of code:

```python
def sigmoid(t):
    return 1/(1+np.exp(-t))


def sigmoid_derivate(p):
    return sigmoid(p) * sigmoid(1-p)
```

Click on the run button.

Next, we will program the feedforward function (see figure 15).

Add the following lines of code:

```python
#Nos proporciona los datos de la capa anterior a la siguiente
def feedforward(X_input):
    #np.dot regresa el producto punto de dos arreglos
    global a0,z0,a1,z1,a2
    a0 = X_input # entrada de datos, no aumenta o decrementa los pesos
    z0 = np.dot(a0,w0) # guarda el acumulado
    a1 = sigmoid(z0) # Formula de activación de la capa
    z1 = np.dot(a1,w1)
    a2 = sigmoid(z1)
    output = a2
    return output
```

Click on the run button

Next, we will program the backpropagation function,

Add the following lines of code:

```
#  Nos proporciona los datos para la capa siguiente

def backprop():


    #Aplicando la regla de la cadena para la funcion de perdida a los pesos 2 y 1

    # T devuelve la matriz traspuesta

    global w0,w1,w2,b0,b1,b2

    mse = np.sum((y - output)**2)

    error.append(mse)

    delta1 = -(y - output) * sigmoid_derivate(z1)

    d_w1 =np.dot(a1.T,delta1)

    d_b1 = delta1


    delta0 = np.dot(delta1,w1.T)* sigmoid_derivate(z0)

    d_w0 = np.dot(a0.T, delta0)

    d_b0 = delta0


    w1= w1 -lr * d_w1

    w0= w0 -lr * d_w0
```

Click on the run button

Next, we will train the neural network with 200 epochs.

Add the following lines of code:

```
for i in range(200):

    output = feedforward(X)

    backprop()

    if i % 10 == 0 :

        print ("Epoch: {}, mse: {}".format(i,error[-1]))
```

Click on the run button, it should look something like this:

```
Epoch: 0, mse: 2.244643726482458
Epoch: 10, mse: 1.975452034687431
Epoch: 20, mse: 1.9641015379246798
Epoch: 30, mse: 1.9527136650429864
Epoch: 40, mse: 1.9387755664634165
```

Epoch: 50, mse: 1.9206708098384495
Epoch: 60, mse: 1.8974052791837055
Epoch: 70, mse: 1.868429426350096
Epoch: 80, mse: 1.8335723684900127
Epoch: 90, mse: 1.7930338899296947
Epoch: 100, mse: 1.7474025933104411
Epoch: 110, mse: 1.6976224915601976
Epoch: 120, mse: 1.6448362394839022
Epoch: 130, mse: 1.5901319284398507
Epoch: 140, mse: 1.5342883832264649
Epoch: 150, mse: 1.47759329504335
Epoch: 160, mse: 1.4197725355184556
Epoch: 170, mse: 1.36006157382125
Epoch: 180, mse: 1.297453152314923
Epoch: 190, mse: 1.2311351753589428

Next, we will display the weights of w0, add the following line of code:

```
w0
```

Click on the run button, it should look something like this:

```
array([[[ 3.09045348, 0.3381738 , 4.54875063, -0.07219332],
    [-0.76271849, 1.11348503, 3.87093059, 1.91943018],
    [-2.67995886, -2.1815292 , -5.95016862, -0.61430587]]])
```

Next, we will do the same with w1, add the following line of code:

```
w1
```

Click on the run button, it should look something like this:

```
array([[[-2.38649282],
    [-1.86736127],
    [ 4.39840749],
    [-1.09890991]]])
```

Next, we will test the model with an approximation

Add the following line of code:

```
output = feedforward([0,0,0])

output
```

Click on the run button, it should look something like this:

```
array([0.38291866])
```

Finally, we will test for the quadratic error of the model

Add the following line of code:

```python
import matplotlib.pyplot as plt
%matplotlib inline
plt.plot(error)
```

Click on the run button, it should look like the one shown in figure 18.

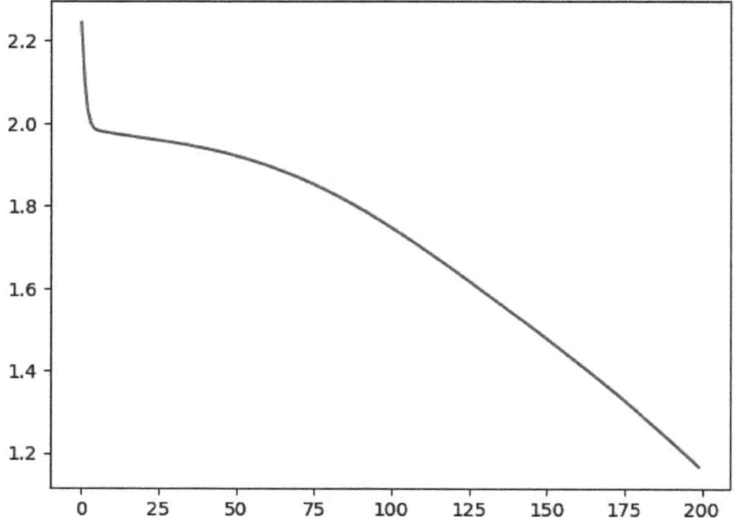

Figure 18. Quadratic error

You can download the source code for this exercise at the following address:

https://github.com/jeliecergomez/Machine_Learning/blob/main/Funcion_XOR.ipynb

End of exercise.

Classification of blight blight in potato images

Objective: To implement a convolutional neural network model that allows the prediction of potato leaf health status as a function of blight disease.

Part I. Contextualization of the problem

The problem:

Potato late blight, caused by the pathogen Phytophthora infestans, represents one of the most devastating threats to potato crops globally. This microorganism can spread rapidly under favorable climatic conditions, causing considerable losses in production and endangering the food security of millions of people around the world. In this text, we will discuss how convolutional neural networks (CNNs) have emerged as a promising tool in the early detection and effective management of potato late blight. The basic principles of CNNs, their implementation in precision agriculture, and their ability to address the challenges associated with this disease will be explored.

Brief definition of late blight

Potato late blight is a fungal disease that can damage all parts of the potato plant, including leaves, stems and tubers. Its characteristic symptoms include dark, wet spots on leaves, which gradually spread and can lead to leaf drop. In addition to direct crop damage, this disease can have a considerable economic impact due to the need for costly control measures, such as regular fungicide application. Effective prevention and management of this disease is essential to ensure food security and sustainability of potato production on a global scale (Yuen, 2021; Paluchowska et al., 2022; Gold et al.,2020).

Convolutional Neural Networks

Convolutional neural networks are a specialized type of deep learning model designed specifically for image analysis. These networks consist of layers of neurons arranged in three dimensions: width, height and depth. When an image is fed into the input layer of a CNN, it goes through a sequence of convolutional and clustering layers, followed by fully connected layers, before generating a classified output. The effectiveness of CNNs is founded on their ability to automatically learn relevant image features, such as edges, textures, and patterns, without requiring manual feature extraction (Li et al.,2021; Lindsay et al., 2021).

Convolutional neural networks (CNNs) have a wide variety of applications in agriculture, ranging from plant disease detection to crop growth monitoring. Specifically in relation to potato late blight, CNNs can be trained to recognize specific patterns in images of plants affected by the disease, facilitating early and accurate detection (Lindsay et al., 2021).

Applications of convolutional neural networks to agriculture.

Disease Detection: CNNs can be trained using images of both healthy and diseased potato plants, allowing them to identify patterns associated with late blight. Once trained, these networks can analyze new images and automatically classify whether a plant is infected or not, allowing early detection and rapid response to disease outbreaks (Chen et al., 2021).

Crop Growth Monitoring: CNNs can also be employed to monitor the growth of potato crops and detect signs of stress or disease. By analyzing images of plants at different stages of development, these networks can identify patterns that indicate healthy growth or potential problems that require attention (Ilesanmi et al., 2021).

Optimizing Resource Use: By providing detailed information on crop status, CNNs can help farmers optimize the use of resources such as water, fertilizers and pesticides. By identifying specific areas of fields that need treatment, these networks can reduce waste and minimize the environmental impact of farming.

Training Convolutional Neural Networks for Potato Late Blight Detection

The effective process of training a CNN to detect potato late blight involves a number of fundamental steps, including data collection and preparation, network design and configuration, and model evaluation and tuning (Kang et al., 2023; Qi et al., 2023). These steps are detailed below:

Data Collection and Preparation: The first step is to collect a data set of images representing both healthy and diseased potato plants. These images should be of high quality and reflect actual conditions. It is crucial to label each image with its corresponding class (i.e., healthy or diseased) to facilitate supervised training of the network.

Network Design and Configuration: Once the data has been collected, the CNN is designed and configured. This involves selecting the appropriate network architecture, including the number and type of convolutional layers, as well as the activation function and regularization parameters. In addition, model hyperparameters, such as learning rate and batch size, which influence model performance and convergence during training, are defined (Qi et al., 2023).

Model Training and Evaluation: Once the network architecture and hyperparameters are defined, the model is trained using the prepared dataset. During this process, the CNN automatically adjusts the weights of the connections between neurons to minimize a loss function that quantifies the discrepancy between the model predictions and the actual image labels. Subsequently, the model is evaluated using a separate test dataset to measure its accuracy and performance in detecting potato late blight.

Model Tuning and Optimization: In case the model does not achieve the desired performance during the evaluation, additional adjustments can be made to the network architecture and hyperparameters to improve its performance.

In view of the above, we will implement a convolutional neural network model for blight pest detection in potato crop.

Part II. Solution development
Next, create a new project in notebook

Click on the file menu, notebook, as shown in figure 19.

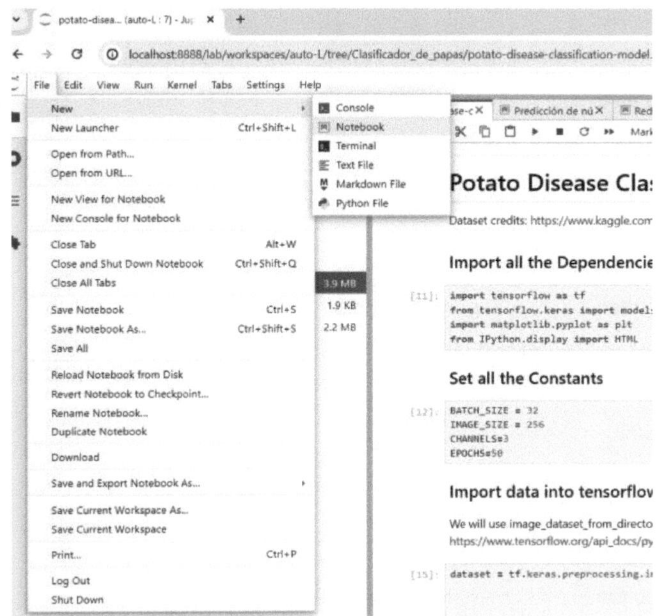

Figure 19, Creating a new project in Jupyter Notebook

Next, select the Python 3 Kernel, as shown in Figure 20.

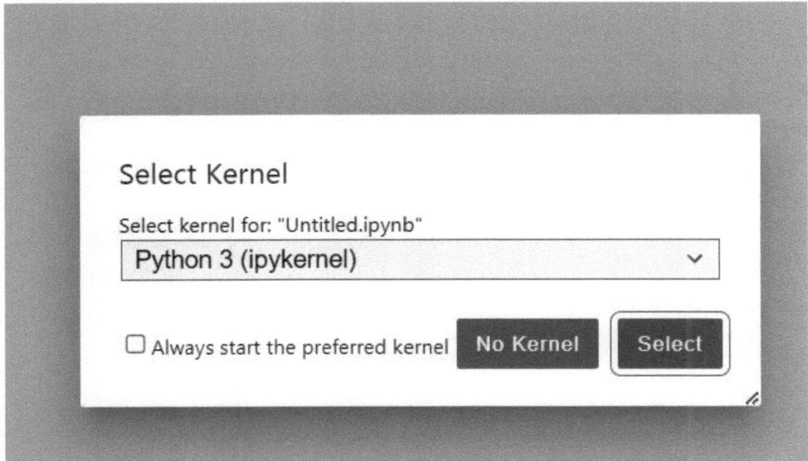

Figure 20. Kernel selection

This exercise is adapted from: https://github.com/codebasics/potato-disease-classification/blob/main/training/potato-disease-classification-model.ipynb

Next, all dependencies will be imported, add the following lines of code

```
import tensorflow as tf

from tensorflow.keras import models, layers

import matplotlib.pyplot as plt
```

Click on the run button.

Next, the constants will be defined, add the following lines of code:

```
BATCH_SIZE = 32

IMAGE_SIZE = 256

CHANNELS=3

EPOCHS=50
```

Click on the run button.

Next, we import data to the tensorflow dataset object

Note: this data can be downloaded directly from
https://www.kaggle.com/datasets/aarishasifkhan/plantvillage-potato-disease-dataset.

To work directly from your computer, download from the website according to the link above, as shown in figure 21.

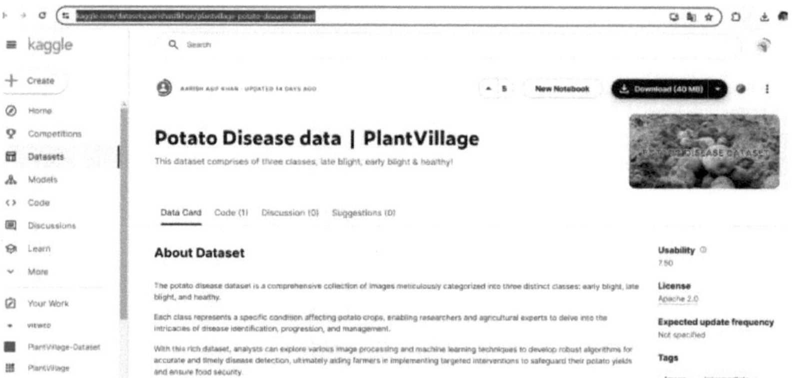

Figure 21. Download of the potato disease dataset.

Next, in the folder where you manage your learning models, add the folder plantvillage, unzip and copy the folder potato, as shown in figure 22.

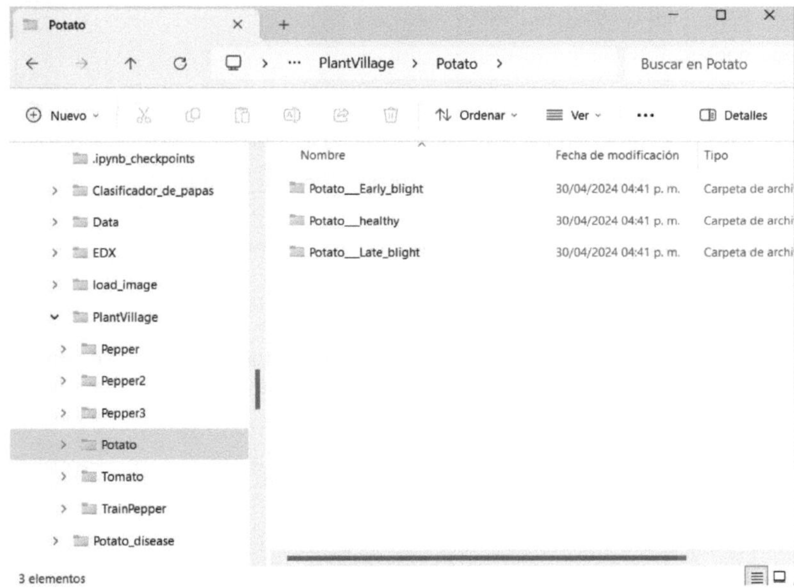

Figure 22. Directory where the images for potato leaf training will be stored.

Then add the following lines of code:

```
dataset =
tf.keras.preprocessing.image_dataset_from_directory("/UCordoba/Machine_Learni
ng/PlantVillage/Potato/",
        seed=123,
        shuffle=True,
        image_size = (IMAGE_SIZE,IMAGE_SIZE),
        batch_size = BATCH_SIZE
        )
```

Click on the run button, this will load the images into the dataset. Note that you must change the location, where you have the images stored.

Next, we will observe the classes that the dataset has defined, to do so, add the following lines of code:

```
class_names = dataset.class_names

class_names
```

Click on the run button, you should get something like this

['Potato___Early_blight', 'Potato___Late_blight', 'Potato___healthy']

Three classes are presented here, namely 'Potato___Early_blight', 'Potato___Late_blight' and 'Potato___healthy'.

Next, we will visualize each element of the dataset is a tuple. The first element is a batch of 32 image elements. The second element is a batch of 32 class label elements.

Add the following lines of code:

```
for image_batch, labels_batch in dataset.take(1):

  print(image_batch.shape)

  print(labels_batch.numpy())
```

Click on the run button, it should look something like this:

(32, 256, 256, 3)
[1 1 1 0 0 0 0 0 1 1 1 0 1 0 1 1 1 0 1 0 1 0 0 1 0 0 1 1 2 0 0]

Some of the images from our dataset are shown below.

Add the following lines of code:

```
plt.figure(figsize=(10, 10))

for image_batch, labels_batch in dataset.take(1):

 for i in range(12):

  ax = plt.subplot(3, 4, i + 1)

  plt.imshow(image_batch[i].numpy().astype("uint8"))

  plt.title(class_names[labels_batch[i]])

  plt.axis("off")
```

Click on the run button, some images should appear, as shown in figure 23.

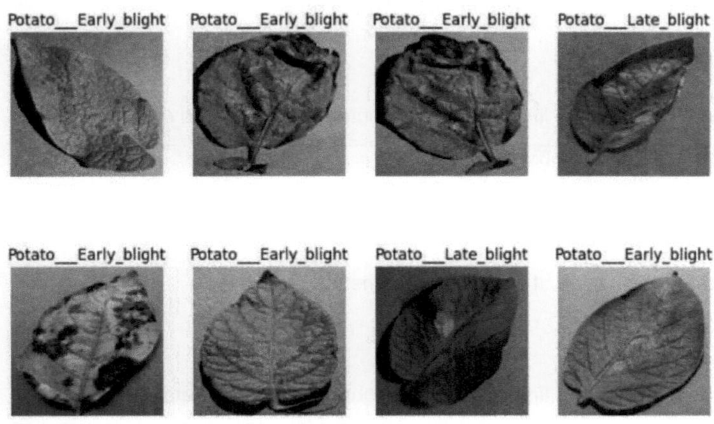

Figure 23. Visualization of dataset images

Next, the function to split the data set will be defined. The data set should be divided into 3 subsets, namely:

- Training: data set to be used during training.
- Validation: set of data to be tested during training
- Test: set of data to be tested after training a model

But first we will look at some values:

Add the following lines of code:

```
len(dataset)
```

Click on the run button and you should get something like this:

68

Add the following lines of code, to define the size of the training, which for this case is 80%.

```
train_size = 0.8
len(dataset)*train_size
```

Click on the run button, it should look something like this:

54.400000000000006

Then add the following lines of code to round up the training data

```
train_ds = dataset.take(54)
len(train_ds)
```

Click on the run button, it should look something like this:

54

Then add the following lines of code, to round up the test data

```
test_ds = dataset.skip(54)
len(test_ds)
```

Click on the run button, it should look something like this:

14

Then add the following lines of code to the validation size

```
val_size=0.1
len(dataset)*val_size
```

Click on the run button, it should look something like this:

6.800000000000001

Then add the following line of code for the validation size of the dataset.

```
val_ds = test_ds.take(6)

len(val_ds)
```

Click on the run button, it should look something like this:

6

Then add the following lines of code to round up the test data

```
test_ds = test_ds.skip(6)

len(test_ds)
```

Click on run

It should look something like this:

8

Next, we will partition the dataset by adding the following lines of code:

```python
def get_dataset_partitions_tf(ds, train_split=0.8, val_split=0.1, test_split=0.1,
shuffle=True, shuffle_size=10000):
 assert (train_split + test_split + val_split) == 1

 ds_size = len(ds)

 if shuffle:
  ds = ds.shuffle(shuffle_size, seed=12)

 train_size = int(train_split * ds_size)
 val_size = int(val_split * ds_size)

 train_ds = ds.take(train_size)
 val_ds = ds.skip(train_size).take(val_size)
 test_ds = ds.skip(train_size).skip(val_size)

 return train_ds, val_ds, test_ds
```

Click on the run button

Next we will assign to the training, test and validation data the partitioning function by adding the following lines of code:

```python
train_ds, val_ds, test_ds = get_dataset_partitions_tf(dataset)
```

Click on the run button

Next, we will display the size of the training data according to the partitioning function, add the following line of code:

```python
len(train_ds)
```

Click on the run button, it should look something like this:

54

We will do the same with the validation data, add the following line of code:

```
len(val_ds)
```

Click on the run button, it should look something like this:

6

Similarly for test data, add the following line of code:

```
len(test_ds)
```

Click on the run button, it should look something like this:

8

The data set will then be cached, shuffled, and pre-captured.

Add the following lines of code:

```
train_ds = train_ds.cache().shuffle(1000).prefetch(buffer_size=tf.data.AUTOTUNE)
val_ds = val_ds.cache().shuffle(1000).prefetch(buffer_size=tf.data.AUTOTUNE)
test_ds = test_ds.cache().shuffle(1000).prefetch(buffer_size=tf.data.AUTOTUNE)
```

Click on the run button.

Model construction. The first thing to do is to create a layer for resizing and normalizing, before sending our images to the network, we must resize them to the desired size. Also, to improve the performance of the model, we must normalize the pixel value of the image (keeping them in the range 0 and 1 by dividing by 256). This should happen both during training and during inference. Therefore, we can add that as a layer in our Sequential Model.

You may be wondering why we should resize the image back to (256,256) if it is already at that size. You are right, it is not strictly necessary to do so, but it will come in handy when we finish the training process and start using the model to make predictions. At that time, it could happen that someone provides an image that is not of dimensions (256,256), and this resizing layer will take care of adjusting it to that size.

Then add the following lines of code:

```
data_augmentation = tf.keras.Sequential([
layers.experimental.preprocessing.RandomFlip("horizontal_and_vertical"),
layers.experimental.preprocessing.RandomRotation(0.2),
])
```

Click on the run button.

Next, we will apply data augmentation to the training dataset, add the following lines of code:

```
train_ds = train_ds.map(

 lambda x, y: (data_augmentation(x, training=True), y)

).prefetch(buffer_size=tf.data.AUTOTUNE)
```

 Click on the run button.

A CNN is used for the model architecture along with a Softmax activation function in the output layer. We also added the initial layers for resizing, normalization and data augmentation.

Then add the following lines of code:

```python
input_shape = (BATCH_SIZE, IMAGE_SIZE, IMAGE_SIZE, CHANNELS)
n_classes = 3 # Para nuestro caso, son tres clases


model = models.Sequential([
resize_and_rescale,
layers.Conv2D(32, kernel_size = (3,3), activation='relu', input_shape=input_shape
layers.MaxPooling2D((2, 2)),
layers.Conv2D(64, kernel_size = (3,3), activation='relu'),
layers.MaxPooling2D((2, 2)),
layers.Conv2D(64, kernel_size = (3,3), activation='relu'),
layers.MaxPooling2D((2, 2)),
layers.Conv2D(64, (3, 3), activation='relu'),
layers.MaxPooling2D((2, 2)),
layers.Conv2D(64, (3, 3), activation='relu'),
layers.MaxPooling2D((2, 2)),
layers.Conv2D(64, (3, 3), activation='relu'),
layers.MaxPooling2D((2, 2)),
layers.Flatten(),
layers.Dense(64, activation='relu'),
layers.Dense(n_classes, activation='softmax'),
])
```

Click on the run button.

Then add the following line of code, to see the summary of the model:

```python
model.summary()
```

Click on the run button, it should look something like this:

Model: "sequential_2"

```
Layer (type) Output Shape Param #
=================================================================
sequential (Sequential) (32, 256, 256, 3) 0
```

conv2d (Conv2D) (32, 254, 254, 32) 896

max_pooling2d (MaxPooling2 (32, 127, 127, 32) 0
D)

conv2d_1 (Conv2D) (32, 125, 125, 64) 18496

max_pooling2d_1 (MaxPoolin (32, 62, 62, 64) 0
g2D)

conv2d_2 (Conv2D) (32, 60, 60, 64) 36928

max_pooling2d_2 (MaxPoolin (32, 30, 30, 64) 0
g2D)

conv2d_3 (Conv2D) (32, 28, 28, 64) 36928

max_pooling2d_3 (MaxPoolin (32, 14, 14, 64) 0
g2D)

conv2d_4 (Conv2D) (32, 12, 12, 64) 36928

max_pooling2d_4 (MaxPoolin (32, 6, 6, 64) 0
g2D)

conv2d_5 (Conv2D) (32, 4, 4, 64) 36928

max_pooling2d_5 (MaxPoolin (32, 2, 2, 64) 0
g2D)

flatten (Flatten) (32, 256) 0

dense (Dense) (32, 64) 16448

dense_1 (Dense) (32, 3) 195

===
Total params: 183747 (717.76 KB)
Trainable params: 183747 (717.76 KB)
Non-trainable params: 0 (0.00 Byte)

Next, we will compile the model, for that purpose we use Adam Optimizer, SparseCategoricalCrossentropy for losses, precision as a metric.

Add the following lines of code:

```python
model.compile(
 optimizer='adam',
 loss=tf.keras.losses.SparseCategoricalCrossentropy(from_logits=False),
 metrics=['accuracy']
)
```

Click on the run button.

Next, we will train the model, add the following lines of code:

```python
history = model.fit(
 train_ds,
 batch_size=BATCH_SIZE,
 validation_data=val_ds,
 verbose=1,
 epochs=50,
)
```

Click on the run button, it should look something like this:

```
Epoch 1/50
54/54 [==============================] - 54s 985ms/step - loss: 0.0296
- accuracy: 0.9896 - val_loss: 0.0206 - val_accuracy: 0.9948
Epoch 2/50
54/54 [==============================] - 27s 484ms/step - loss: 0.0200
- accuracy: 0.9954 - val_loss: 0.3306 - val_accuracy: 0.9375
Epoch 3/50
54/54 [==============================] - 24s 447ms/step - loss: 0.0180
- accuracy: 0.9936 - val_loss: 0.2203 - val_accuracy: 0.9479
Epoch 4/50
54/54 [==============================] - 27s 502ms/step - loss: 0.0170
- accuracy: 0.9942 - val_loss: 0.0328 - val_accuracy: 0.9844
Epoch 5/50
54/54 [==============================] - 28s 514ms/step - loss: 0.0241
- accuracy: 0.9902 - val_loss: 0.0274 - val_accuracy: 0.9896
Epoch 6/50
54/54 [==============================] - 29s 540ms/step - loss: 0.0333
- accuracy: 0.9896 - val_loss: 0.3130 - val_accuracy: 0.9167
.

.

.
```

Epoch 49/50
54/54 [==============================] - 32s 597ms/step - loss: 0.0080 - accuracy: 0.9971 - val_loss: 0.0128 - val_accuracy: 1.0000
Epoch 50/50
54/54 [==============================] - 32s 597ms/step - loss: 0.0202 - accuracy: 0.9954 - val_loss: 0.0012 - val_accuracy: 1.0000

[49]:
```
scores = model.evaluate(test_ds)
```
As can be seen that an accuracy of 100.00% is obtained for our test data set. This is considered a fairly good accuracy.

Next, we will display the training score by adding the following line of code:

```
scores
```

Click on the run button, it should look something like this:

[0.040544070303440094, 0.99609375]

The scores are only a list containing loss and accuracy values.

Next, we will visualize the precision and loss curves by adding the following line of code:

```
history
```

Click on the run button

Next, we will show the history parameters, add the following line of code:

```
history.params
```

Click on the run button, it should look something like this:

{'verbose': 1, 'epochs': 50, 'steps': 54}

Then add the following line of code:

```
history.history.keys()
```

Click on the run button, it should look something like this:

dict_keys(['loss', 'accuracy', 'val_loss', 'val_accuracy'])

The result displays the loss, precision, value loss, among others. are a Python list containing values for loss, precision, etc. at the end of each epoch.

Then add the following line of code:

```
type(history.history['loss'])
```

Click on the run button, it should look something like this:

list

Then add the following line of code to the number of losses

```
len(history.history['loss'])
```

Click on the run button, it should look something like this:

50

Then add the following line of code, to show the loss of the first five epochs

```
history.history['loss'][:5] # show loss for first 5 epochs
```

Click on the run button, it should look something like this:

```
[0.02961837127804756,
 0.020013125613331795,
 0.018016580492258072,
 0.016978314146399498,
 0.024131562560796738]
```

Next, we will calculate the precision and loss for the validation data. Add the following lines of code:

```
acc = history.history['accuracy']

val_acc = history.history['val_accuracy']


loss = history.history['loss']

val_loss = history.history['val_loss']
```

Click on the run button.

Next, we will visualize the training and validation curves for accuracy and loss. Add the following lines of code:

```
plt.figure(figsize=(8, 8))
plt.subplot(1, 2, 1)
plt.plot(range(EPOCHS), acc, label='Training Accuracy')
plt.plot(range(EPOCHS), val_acc, label='Validation Accuracy')
plt.legend(loc='lower right')
plt.title('Training and Validation Accuracy')


plt.subplot(1, 2, 2)
plt.plot(range(EPOCHS), loss, label='Training Loss')
plt.plot(range(EPOCHS), val_loss, label='Validation Loss')
plt.legend(loc='upper right')
plt.title('Training and Validation Loss')
plt.show()
```

Click on the run button, it should look something like the one shown in figure 24.

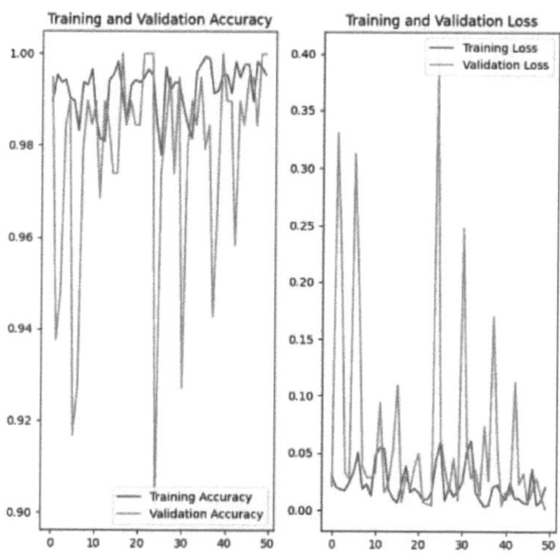

Figure 24. Loss and validation curves in training

Next, we will display a test image by adding the following lines of code:

```python
import numpy as np

for images_batch, labels_batch in test_ds.take(1):


    first_image = images_batch[0].numpy().astype('uint8')
    first_label = labels_batch[0].numpy()


    print("first image to predict")
    plt.imshow(first_image)
    print("actual label:",class_names[first_label])


    batch_prediction = model.predict(images_batch)
    print("predicted label:",class_names[np.argmax(batch_prediction[0])])
```

Click on the run button, it should look something like the one shown in figure 25.

```
first image to predict
current label: Potato___Early_blight
1/1 [==============================] - 0s 278ms/step
predicted label: Potato___Early_blight
```

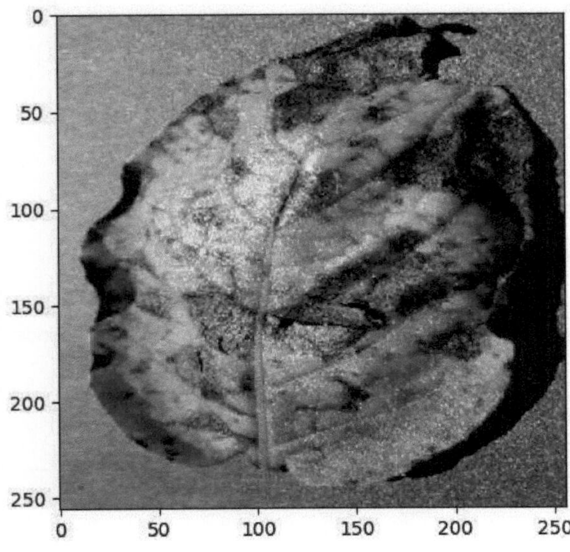

Figure 25. First image of the predictor.

Next, we will write the model inference function. Add the following lines of code:

```python
def predict(model, img):
 img_array = tf.keras.preprocessing.image.img_to_array(images[i].numpy())
 img_array = tf.expand_dims(img_array, 0)

 predictions = model.predict(img_array)

 predicted_class = class_names[np.argmax(predictions[0])]
 confidence = round(100 * (np.max(predictions[0])), 2)
 return predicted_class, confidence
```

Click on the run button.

Next, we will test the model with a certain number of images, which will allow us to predict the health status of potato leaves.

Add the following lines of code:

```python
plt.figure(figsize=(15, 15))
for images, labels in test_ds.take(1):
 for i in range(9):
  ax = plt.subplot(3, 3, i + 1)
  plt.imshow(images[i].numpy().astype("uint8"))

  predicted_class, confidence = predict(model, images[i].numpy())
  actual_class = class_names[labels[i]]

  plt.title(f"Actual:  {actual_class},\n  Predicted:  {predicted_class}.\n  Confidence:
{confidence}%")

  plt.axis("off")
```

Click on the run button, it should look something like the one shown in figure 26.

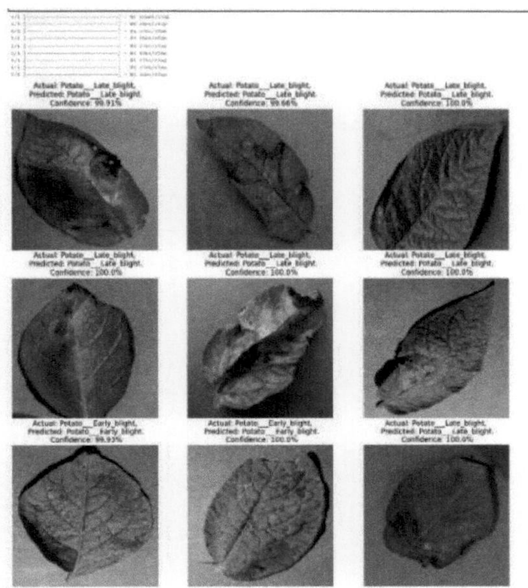

Figure 26. Prediction of potato leaf health status.

Finally, we will save the model for later use in a web or mobile application.

Add the following lines of code:

```
import os
model_version=max([int(i) for i in os.listdir("/UCordoba/Machine_Learning/Clasificador_de_papas/models/") + [0]])+1
model.save(f"/UCordoba/Machine_Learning/Clasificador_de_papas/models/{model_version}")
```

Click on the run button.

For the previous lines of code, what is intended is to iteratively create folders that save the version of the model. That is, each time you update the model epochs, a new version is created, as shown in Figure 27.

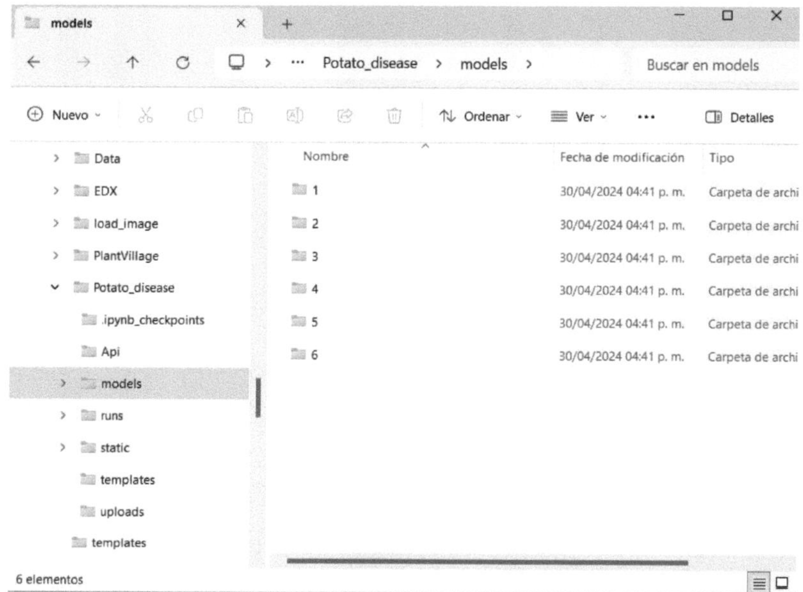

Figure 27. Stored models.

As shown in Figure 27, each time we update or run new epochs in the model, the model stores the version of each epoch.

In the event that you only need the latest version, you can do so by adding the following code:

```
model.save("/UCordoba/Machine_Learning/Clasificador_de_papas/potatoes.h5")
```

Click on the run button, this will allow storing the trained model.

If you want to access the code of this guide, please follow this link :

https://github.com/jeliecergomez/Machine_Learning/blob/main/Potato_disease/Training.ipynb

Web application development in Flask

To use the pre-trained model we will develop a web application, which uses the model, loads the image, makes the prediction and displays the predicted image on the web page.

Initially we will install the Flask server in Python, which allows us to create servers without so many complications.

To do this you must install the Flask package. Then go to the command lines in Windows, as shown in Figure 28, and type the following command:

```
pip install flask
```

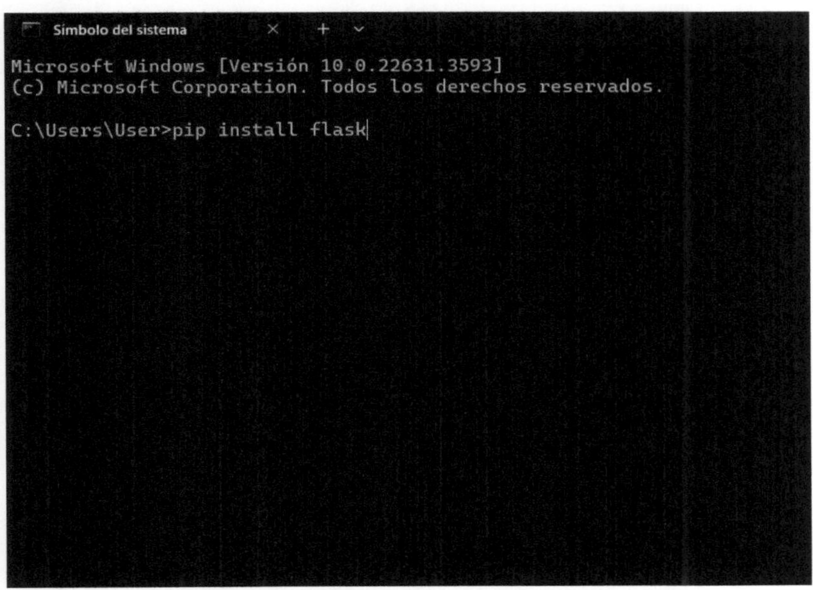

Figure 28. Command line to install Flask

For the operation of the server and the applications, the following directory structure is required as shown in Figure 29.

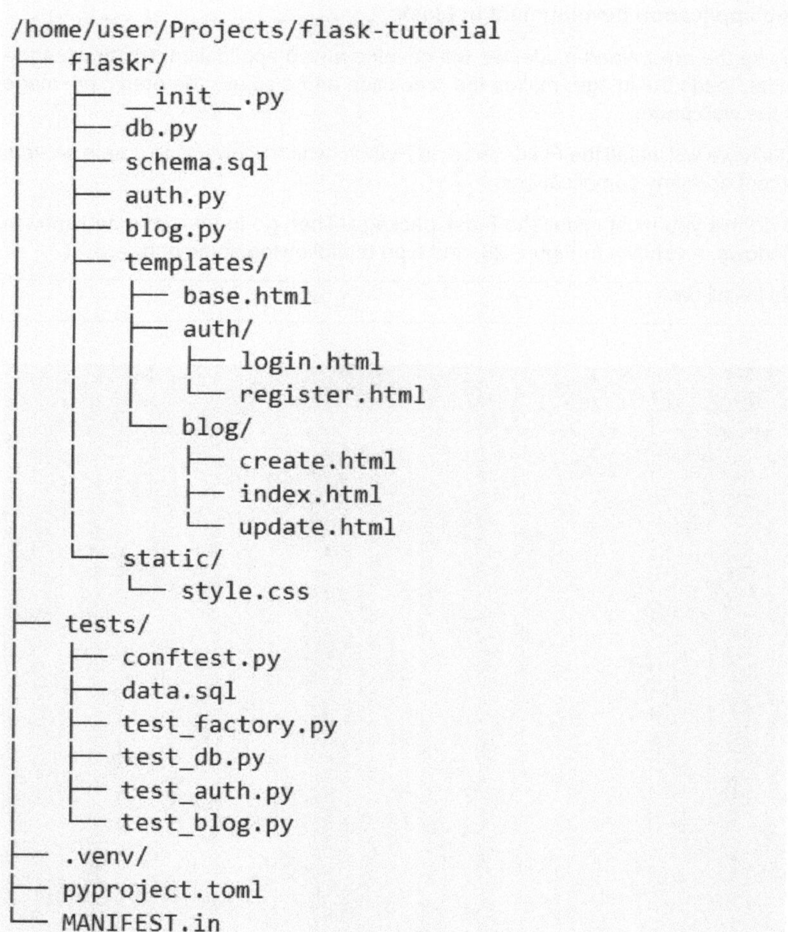

```
/home/user/Projects/flask-tutorial
├── flaskr/
│   ├── __init__.py
│   ├── db.py
│   ├── schema.sql
│   ├── auth.py
│   ├── blog.py
│   ├── templates/
│   │   ├── base.html
│   │   ├── auth/
│   │   │   ├── login.html
│   │   │   └── register.html
│   │   └── blog/
│   │       ├── create.html
│   │       ├── index.html
│   │       └── update.html
│   └── static/
│       └── style.css
├── tests/
│   ├── conftest.py
│   ├── data.sql
│   ├── test_factory.py
│   ├── test_db.py
│   ├── test_auth.py
│   └── test_blog.py
├── .venv/
├── pyproject.toml
└── MANIFEST.in
```

Figure 29. Directory structure for Flask

For the case of this project, in the root directory, we will place the file of the pre-trained model called potatoes.h5

Our directory will be organized as follows, as shown in Figure 30.

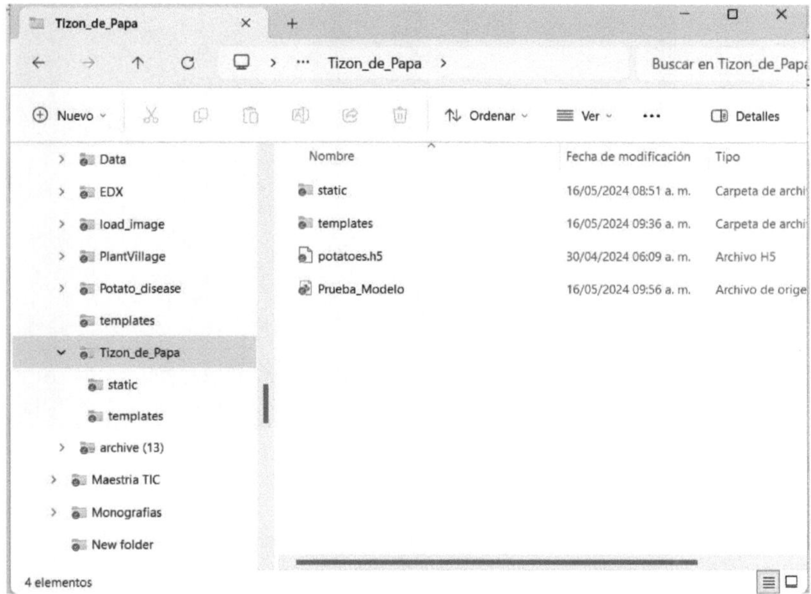

Figure 30. Directory for the potato leaf sorting web server.

As shown in the previous figure, you must create a folder with the name Tizon_de_Papa

In the folder of Tizon_de_Papa, create the static subfolders, which will allow to host the images that are loaded from its invocation to later visualize them in the web page.

In the same way create the subfolder templates, where we will store the index.html

Once these directories have been created, we proceed to code the instructions to access the server and deploy the web application. Next, we open visual code studio to create the code that will allow us to run the website. Click on file -> new file, and store in the path of Tizon_de_Papa the name of the file Prueba modelo and click on create new file, as shown in figure 31.

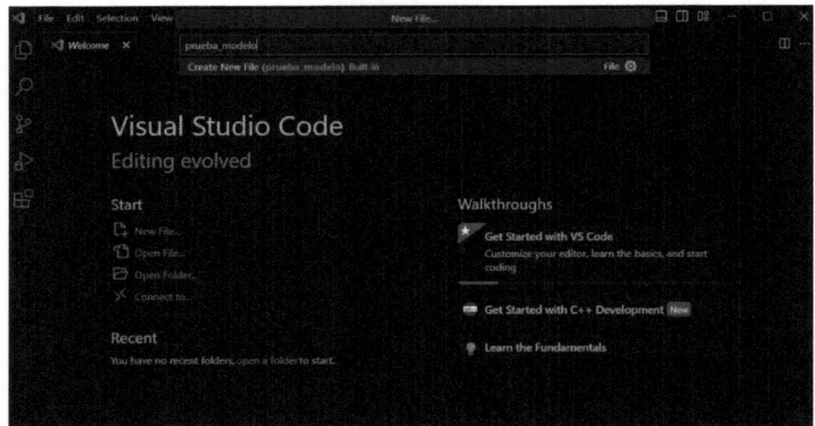

Figure 31. Creating the server application

Next, locate the file in the folder mentioned above, as shown in Figure 32.

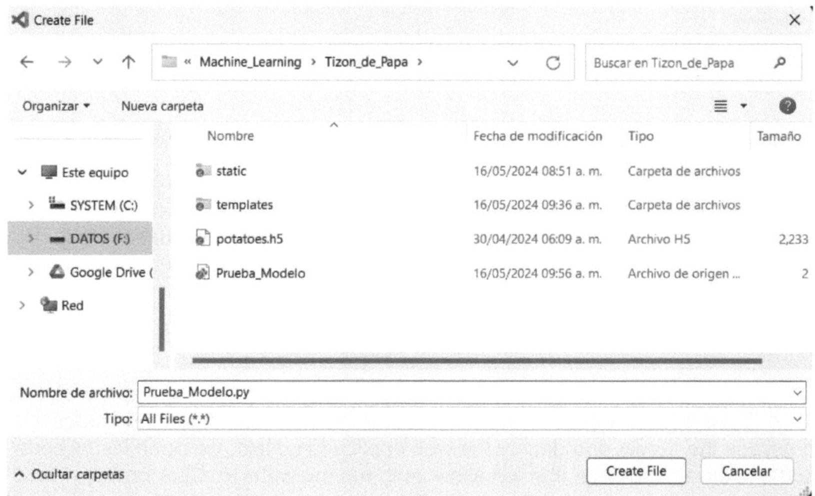

Figure 32. Saving the model

Then, in the body text of the file, add the following lines of code:

```python
# Import necessary libraries
from flask import Flask, render_template, request
from keras.models import load_model
from PIL import Image
import numpy as np


# Initialize Flask app
app = Flask(__name__)

# Load pre-trained model
model = load_model('/UCordoba/Machine_Learning/Potato_disease/potatoes.h5')

# Define function to preprocess image
def preprocess_image(image_path):
 img = Image.open(image_path)
 img = img.resize((256, 256)) # Resize image to match model input shape
 img_array = np.array(img) / 255.0 # Normalize pixel values
 img_array = np.expand_dims(img_array, axis=0) # Add batch dimension
 return img_array

# Define function to make prediction
def predict_image(image_path):
 img_array = preprocess_image(image_path)
 prediction = model.predict(img_array)
 classes = ["Early Blight", "Late Blight", "Healthy"]
 predicted_class = classes[np.argmax(prediction)]
 return predicted_class


# Define route for home page
@app.route('/', methods=['GET', 'POST'])
def home():
 if request.method == 'POST':
  if 'file' not in request.files:
   return render_template('index.html', error="No file part")
  file = request.files['file']
  if file.filename == '':
   return render_template('index.html', error="No selected file")
  if file:
   # Save uploaded image
   image_path = "/UCordoba/Machine_Learning/Potato_disease/static/" + file.filename
   file.save(image_path)
   # Make prediction
# Run Flask app
if __name__ == '__main__':
 app.run(debug=True)
```

Note: to avoid problems when loading the model as shown in the following line:

```python
# Load pre-trained model
model =load_model('/UCordoba/Machine_Learning/Potato_disease/potatoes.h5')
```

Add the following instruction:

```python
# Load pre-trained model
model =load_model('/UCordoba/Machine_Learning/Potato_disease/potatoes.h5',
compile=False)
```

With this you will be able to run the script without any problem.

The line to load pre-trained model, replace the location where the popatoes.h5 file, which you have on your computer, is located.

```python
# Load pre-trained model
model =load_model('/UCordoba/Machine_Learning/Potato_disease/potatoes.h5')
```

In the same way, change the location to the corresponding location on your computer in the line:

```python
image_path = "/UCordoba/Machine_Learning/Potato_disease/static/" + file.filename
```

of the path definition function for the web page

```python
# Define route for home page
@app.route('/', methods=['GET', 'POST'])
def home():
 if request.method == 'POST':
  if 'file' not in request.files:
   return render_template('index.html', error="No file part")
  file = request.files['file']
  if file.filename == '':
   return render_template('index.html', error="No selected file")
  if file:
   # Save uploaded image
   image_path = "/UCordoba/Machine_Learning/Potato_disease/static/" + file.filename

   file.save(image_path)
   # Make prediction
   prediction = predict_image(image_path)
   return render_template('index.html', prediction=prediction, filenamex=file.filename, imagepath=image_path)
 return render_template('index.html')
```

Once the changes have been made, click on save, as shown in figure 33.

Figure 33. Saving the application.

Next, we will create the web page, with a file called index.html

Again click on file -> new file in visual studio code, as shown in figure 34.

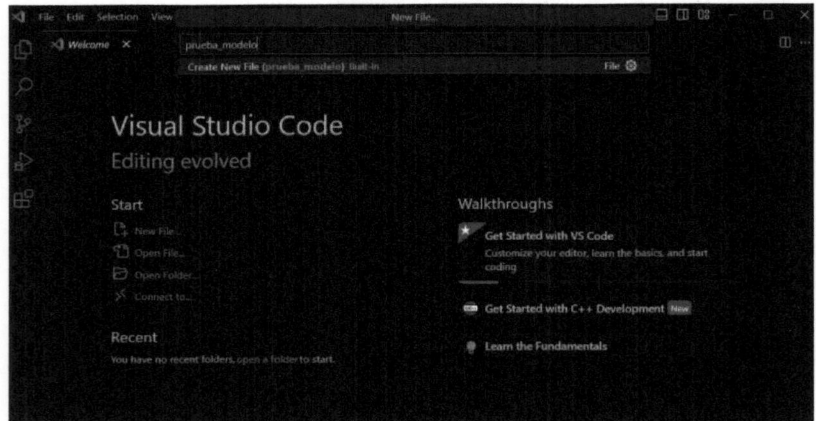

Figure 34. Saving the web page

Then click on Create New File and save the index.html file in the templates folder, as shown in Figure 35.

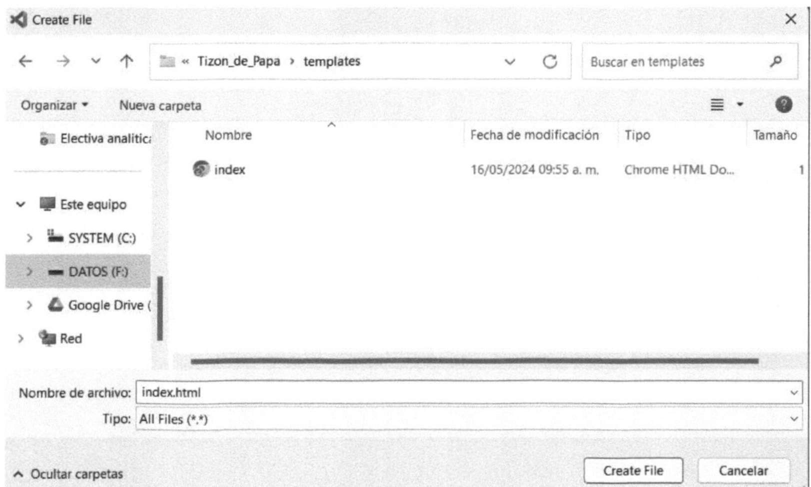

Figure 35. Saving the index.html page in the templates folder.

Then click on the create button.

Then copy this code into the body of the file

```html
<!DOCTYPE html>
<html lang="en">
<head>
 <meta charset="UTF-8">
 <meta name="viewport" content="width=device-width, initial-scale=1.0">
 <title>Clasificador de Imagenes de papa</title>
</head>
<body>
 <h1>Clasificador de Imagenes de papa</h1>
{% if prediction %}
 <h2>Resultado para la imagen: {{ filenamex }}: {{ prediction }}</h2>
 <h2>

 <img src= "{{url_for('static', filename=filenamex)}}" alt="Prediccion de imagen: {{ prediction }}"
style="max-width: 500px"/>
 <h3>
 Prediccion: {{ prediction }}
 </h3>

 </h2>
{% endif %}
 <form method="post" enctype="multipart/form-data">
 <input type="file" name="file">
 <input type="submit" value="Cargar">
 </form>
{% if error %}
 <p>{{ error }}</p>
{% endif %}
</body>
</html>
```

Then press the Ctrl+S key to save the file.

Next, we will run the web application, for this we enter the command line and give the following instruction, as shown in figure 36.

Figure 36. Running the web application.

You must type in the command line:

```
python Prueba_Modelo.py
```

Once the application is executed, the output should look like the one shown in figure 37.

Figure 37. Server deployed

Copy the address http://127.0.0.1:5000 in your browser

You should get something as shown in figure 38.

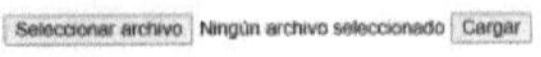

Figure 38. Deployment of the web application in the browser.

Then click the select file button

Next, choose one of the folders containing the three classifications of potato leaves, as shown in Figure 39.

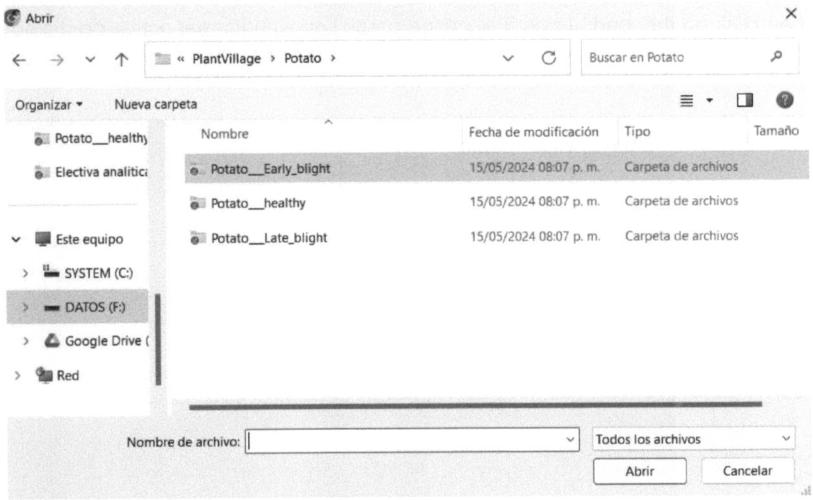

Figure 39. Directory with images of potato leaf classes.

Once you have decided to choose the directory and selected the image, as shown in Figure 40.

65

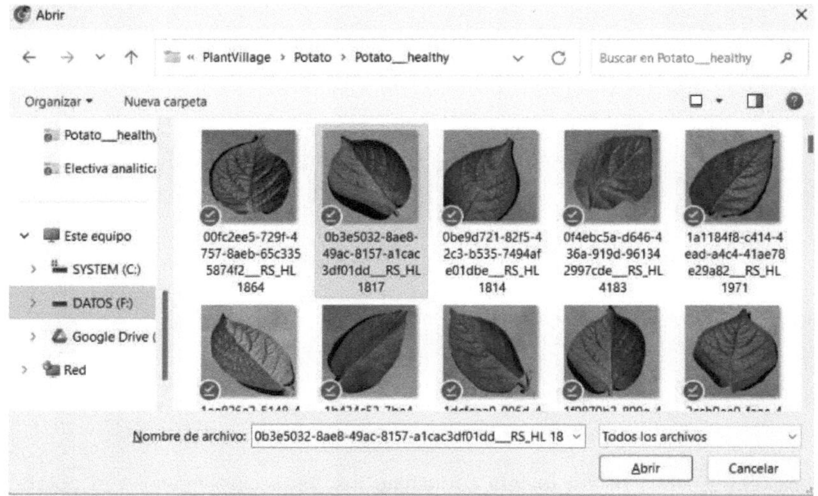

Figure 40. Image selection.

Click on open.

Then click on the load button, the image prediction with its respective predicted health status should appear, as shown in Figures 41, 42 and 43.

Clasificador de Imagenes de papa

Resultado para la imagen: 1b434c52-7be4-40c4-90d5-13220f1a3eba___RS_HL 5418.JPG: Healthy

Figure 41. Healthy image

Clasificador de Imagenes de papa

Resultado para la imagen: 0a6983a5-895e-4e68-9edb-88adf79211e9___RS_Early.B 9072.JPG: Early Blight

Prediccion: Early Blight

Seleccionar archivo | Ningún archivo seleccionado | Cargar

Figure 42. Early diseased image

Clasificador de Imagenes de papa

Resultado para la imagen: 1cffe6a1-6fb3-4506-846c-478148a2b678___RS_LB 4380.JPG: Late Blight

Prediccion: Late Blight

Seleccionar archivo | Ningún archivo seleccionado | Cargar

Figure 43. Totally diseased image.

The complete project can be downloaded from:

https://github.com/jeliecergomez/Machine_Learning/tree/main/Tizon_Papa

Activity.

Download the pepper dataset from the Kaggle website and train the model according to the above guide.

End of the guide

References

Park, Y. S., & Lek, S. (2016). Artificial neural networks: Multilayer perceptron for ecological modeling. In Developments in environmental modelling (Vol. 28, pp. 123-140). Elsevier.

Ma, Z., & Mei, G. (2021). Deep learning for geological hazards analysis: Data, models, applications, and opportunities. Earth-Science Reviews, 223, 103858.

Goldberg, Y. (2016). A primer on neural network models for natural language processing. Journal of Artificial Intelligence Research, 57, 345-420.

Acharya, U. R., Oh, S. L., Hagiwara, Y., Tan, J. H., Adam, M., Gertych, A., & San Tan, R. (2017). A deep convolutional neural network model to classify heartbeats. Computers in biology and medicine, 89, 389-396.

Grossberg, S., & Merrill, J. W. (1992). A neural network model of adaptively timed reinforcement learning and hippocampal dynamics. Cognitive brain research, 1(1), 3-38.

Nagabandi, A., Kahn, G., Fearing, R. S., & Levine, S. (2018, May). Neural network dynamics for model-based deep reinforcement learning with model-free fine-tuning. In 2018 IEEE international conference on robotics and automation (ICRA) (pp. 7559-7566). IEEE.

Canziani, A., Paszke, A., & Culurciello, E. (2016). An analysis of deep neural network models for practical applications. arXiv preprint arXiv:1605.07678.

Schmidhuber, J. (2015). Deep learning in neural networks: An overview. Neural networks, 61, 85-117.

Nielsen, M. A. (2015). Neural networks and deep learning (Vol. 25, pp. 15-24). San Francisco, CA, USA: Determination press.

Montesinos López, O. A., Montesinos López, A., & Crossa, J. (2022). Fundamentals of artificial neural networks and deep learning. In Multivariate statistical machine learning methods for genomic prediction (pp. 379-425). Cham: Springer International Publishing.

Baldi, P., Sadowski, P., & Lu, Z. (2018). Learning in the machine: Random backpropagation and the deep learning channel. Artificial intelligence, 260, 1-35.

Cilimkovic, M. (2015). Neural networks and back propagation algorithm. Institute of Technology Blanchardstown, Blanchardstown Road North Dublin, 15(1).

Liao, R., Xiong, Y., Fetaya, E., Zhang, L., Yoon, K., Pitkow, X., ... & Zemel, R. (2018, July). Reviving and improving recurrent back-propagation. In International Conference on Machine Learning (pp. 3082-3091). PMLR.

Hecht-Nielsen, R. (1992). Theory of the backpropagation neural network. In Neural networks for perception (pp. 65-93). Academic Press.

Badr, A. (2021). Awesome back-propagation machine learning paradigm. Neural Computing and Applications, 33(20), 13225-13249.

Ozanich, E., Gerstoft, P., & Niu, H. (2020). A feedforward neural network for direction-of-arrival estimation. The journal of the acoustical society of America, 147(3), 2035-2048.

Khan, J., Lee, E., & Kim, K. (2023). A higher prediction accuracy-based alpha-beta filter algorithm using the feedforward artificial neural network. CAAI Transactions on Intelligence Technology, 8(4), 1124-1139.

Yuen, J. (2021). Pathogens which threaten food security: Phytophthora infestans, the potato late blight pathogen. Food Security, 13(2), 247-253.

Paluchowska, P., Śliwka, J., & Yin, Z. (2022). Late blight resistance genes in potato breeding. Planta, 255(6), 127.

Gold, K. M., Townsend, P. A., Herrmann, I., & Gevens, A. J. (2020). Investigating potato late blight physiological differences across potato cultivars with spectroscopy and machine learning. Plant Science, 295, 110316.

Li, Z., Liu, F., Yang, W., Peng, S., & Zhou, J. (2021). A survey of convolutional neural networks: analysis, applications, and prospects. IEEE transactions on neural networks and learning systems, 33(12), 6999-7019.

Lindsay, G. W. (2021). Convolutional neural networks as a model of the visual system: Past, present, and future. Journal of cognitive neuroscience, 33(10), 2017-2031.

Chen, L., Li, S., Bai, Q., Yang, J., Jiang, S., & Miao, Y. (2021). Review of image classification algorithms based on convolutional neural networks. Remote Sensing, 13(22), 4712.

Ilesanmi, A. E., & Ilesanmi, T. O. (2021). Methods for image denoising using convolutional neural network: a review. Complex & Intelligent Systems, 7(5), 2179-2198.

Kang, F., Li, J., Wang, C., & Wang, F. (2023). A lightweight neural network-based method for identifying early-blight and late-blight leaves of potato. Applied Sciences, 13(3), 1487.

Qi, C., Sandroni, M., Westergaard, J. C., Sundmark, E. H. R., Bagge, M., Alexandersson, E., & Gao, J. (2023). In-field classification of the asymptomatic biotrophic phase of potato late blight based on deep learning and proximal hyperspectral imaging. Computers and Electronics in Agriculture, 205, 107585.

More
Books!

info@omniscriptum.com
www.omniscriptum.com
OMNIScriptum